THE KOOKY 3D

kids'

BAKING BOOK

THE KOOKY 3D kids' BAKING BOOK

hardie grant books

MELBOURNE · LONDON

CONTENTS

savoury 8

HAM AND PINEAPPLE SCROLLS ● CHEESY TWISTS
JUNGLE MUFFINS ● SO-EASY SAUSAGE ROLLS
DINNER ROLLS ● GARLIC AND HERB PRETZELS
MINI PUMPKIN QUICKBREADS ● COWBOY ROLLS
PESTO PASTRIES ● VEGGIE FILO CUPS
CALZONES ● CHICKEN AND CORN COTTAGE PIES

sweet 34

WHOOPIE PIES ● CHOCCY BUTTERFLY CAKES
JAM THUMBPRINT DROPS ● BAKED DOUGHNUTS
LITTLE FRESH FRUIT TARTS ● CHOCOLATE PROFITEROLES
ORANGE YOYO COOKIES ● MINI BERRY CAKES
RASPBERRY CREAM HORNS ● KOOKY CAKE POPS
ROCKY ROAD CUPS ● ANIMAL COOKIES
SPARKLY MERINGUE KISSES

Are you tired of boring 2D food? Then put on your 3D glasses and watch food come to life!

READ THIS FIRST

Cooking 3D food is not that different from cooking 2D food: you still need to follow some basic kitchen rules. Before you begin, remember to take your 3D glasses off (no wearing them while you're chopping, using equipment or going near the stovetop!). Always ask a grown-up before you start cooking (you don't want to give them a shock when they see the mess!). Ask for help if you need to do anything tricky like chopping, handling hot pans or taking things out of the oven.

Now that we've got the safety tips out of the way, next on the list is hygiene! Wash your hands with soap before you start and try to keep your work area tidy. Keep all meat in the fridge before cooking. When you've chopped raw meat, don't use the same knife and board for other ingredients that are served uncooked, such as salad leaves or fruit.

Read the recipe ALL THE WAY TO THE END before you start cooking. You might discover ingredients or equipment you don't have (and it can be really annoying if you have to pay your younger brother or sister to run to the shop).

All the spoon measures and cup measures are LEVEL so don't use more than the recipe tells you to. One tablespoon is equal to 20 ml or 4 teaspoons. All cake and tart tins are measured across the base, not the top. We use standard 59 g (2¼ oz) eggs in the recipes, and butter is salted unless we say unsalted. If you're using the oven, arrange the shelves before you preheat the oven. A fan-forced oven will be hotter than a normal oven and doesn't need preheating. You'll need to turn your fan-forced oven 10°C (50°F) lower than the temperature in the recipe. Get a grown-up to help you with this.

When you've finished cooking, take a good look, then put on your 3D glasses and compare your dish to the picture. Magic!

SAVOURY

HAM AND PINEAPPLE
scrolls

MAKES 12 I **PREP TIME** 20 MINS I **COOKING TIME** 18–20 MINS

300 g (10^1/2 oz/2 cups) **self-raising flour**
30 g (1 oz) **butter**, chilled and chopped
185 ml (6 fl oz/^{3}/4 cup) **milk**
125 ml (4^1/2 fl oz/^{1}/2 cup) **tomato pasta sauce**
100 g (3^1/2 oz/1 cup) grated **cheddar cheese**
100 g (3^1/2 oz) shaved **ham**, chopped
1 x 440 g (15^1/2 oz) tin **pineapple thins**, well drained and chopped

1 Preheat the oven to 200°C (400°F/Gas 6). Line a large baking tray with baking paper. Sift the flour into a mixing bowl. Add the butter and use your fingertips to rub it into the flour until combined. Make a well in the centre of the flour mixture.

2 Pour the milk into the well. Use a non-serrated knife to mix in the flour until almost combined. With your hands, gather the dough into a ball and turn out onto a lightly floured work surface. Roll out to a rectangle, about 36 x 24 cm (14^1/4 x 9^1/2 inches).

3 Spread the pasta sauce over the dough, leaving a 3 cm (1^1/4 inch) border along both long edges. Sprinkle evenly with the cheese, ham and pineapple. Starting from a long side, roll the dough up firmly like a Swiss roll.

4 Cut the roll into 12 even slices. Arrange the scrolls close together on the tray, making sure the seam ends are turned inwards, so the scrolls don't unroll while cooking. Bake for 18–20 minutes or until golden and cooked through. Serve warm or at room temperature.

CHEESY twists

MAKES 24 | **PREP TIME** 30 MINS + 10 MINS CHILLING | **COOKING TIME** 12–15 MINS

150 g (5$\frac{1}{2}$ oz/1 cup) **plain (all-purpose) flour**
50 g (1$\frac{3}{4}$ oz/$\frac{1}{3}$ cup) **self-raising flour**
100 g (3$\frac{1}{2}$ oz) **butter**, frozen
1 teaspoon **cooking salt**
80 ml (2$\frac{1}{2}$ fl oz/$\frac{1}{3}$ cup) **iced water**
2 tablespoons chopped **chives**
2 tablespoons finely grated **parmesan cheese**

1 Preheat the oven to 190°C (375°F/Gas 5). Line two large baking trays with baking paper. Sift the flours together into a bowl. Coarsely grate the butter over the flour. Stir through along with the salt. Make a well in the centre and add the water. Use a non-serrated knife to mix through until evenly moistened — you may need a little more water. The butter will stay in little lumps, but this is okay. With your hands, gather the dough into a ball and turn out onto a sheet of baking paper.

2 Roll out to a rectangle, about 30 x 25 cm (12 x 10 inches). Sprinkle the chives and cheese evenly over the pastry. Gently roll the rolling pin over the pastry to press the filling in. Cut in half lengthways, then cut each half crossways into 12 strips. Chill for 10 minutes.

3 Lift each strip and place onto the trays, twisting each a couple of times. Bake for 12–15 minutes or until crisp and golden. Transfer to a wire rack to cool.

If you are short of time, use a sheet of thawed frozen puff pastry.

JUNGLE
muffins

MAKES 8 | **PREP TIME** 20 MINS | **COOKING TIME** 25 MINS

375 g (13 oz/2^1/2 cups) **self-raising flour**
2 **eggs**
250 ml (9 fl oz/1 cup) **milk**
125 g (4^1/2 oz) **butter**, melted and cooled
100 g (3^1/2 oz) shaved **salami**, chopped
65 g (2^1/4 oz) **semi-dried (sun-blushed) tomatoes**, chopped
100 g (3^1/2 oz/1 cup) grated **cheddar cheese**
1 x 310 g (11 oz) tin **corn kernels**, drained

1 Preheat the oven to 190°C (375°F/Gas 5). Lightly grease eight 185 ml (6 fl oz/^{3}/4 cup capacity) muffin holes or line with paper cases.

2 Sift the flour into a mixing bowl and make a well in the centre. Whisk the eggs and milk together with a fork. Add to the flour, along with the butter, salami, semi-dried tomato, cheese and corn. Use a rubber spatula to gently fold the ingredients together until just combined.

3 Spoon into the muffin holes. Bake for 25 minutes or until risen, golden and the muffins spring back when gently touched. Leave in the tin for 5 minutes, then transfer to a wire rack. Serve warm or at room temperature.

The muffins may be frozen. Cool completely, then wrap individually in foil. Place in an airtight container or bag to freeze.

SO-EASY
sausage rolls

MAKES 12 | **PREP TIME** 20 MINS | **COOKING TIME** 10 MINS

3 sheets frozen **puff pastry**, thawed
12 **small sausages (chipolatas)**
1 **egg**, lightly beaten
tomato sauce (ketchup), to serve

1 Preheat the oven to 190°C (375°F/Gas 5). Line a large baking tray with a sheet of baking paper. Cut a very thin strip of pastry from each edge of each sheet and set aside for decoration. Cut the remaining pastry sheets into quarters. Place a sausage along one edge of a pastry square, leaving an even amount of space on either side. Roll up to enclose the sausage.

2 Pinch the pastry in firmly at the ends of each sausage, flaring out the ends of the pastry. Roll the reserved pastry strip in a spiral around the sausage. Place, seam-side down, on the tray and brush with the egg. Bake for 10 minutes or until puffed and golden. Serve with the tomato sauce for dipping.

Chipolatas are roughly half the size of a normal sausage, about 7 cm (2 3/4 inches) long.

DINNER **rolls**

MAKES 12 | **PREP TIME** 30 MINS + 1 HOUR 20 MINS RISING | **COOKING TIME** 15 MINS

125 ml (4^{1}/$_{2}$ fl oz/^{1}/$_{2}$ cup) **lukewarm water**
2 teaspoons **instant dried yeast**
1 teaspoon **caster (superfine) sugar**
1 teaspoon **cooking salt**
450 g (1 lb/3 cups) **plain bread (strong) flour**
185 ml (6 fl oz/^{3}/$_{4}$ cup) **lukewarm milk**
milk, extra, to brush
poppy seeds and **sesame seeds**, to sprinkle

1 Combine the water, yeast, sugar and salt in a bowl. Stand for 10 minutes or until the mixture is frothy. Place the flour in a mixing bowl and make a well in the centre. Add the yeast mixture and milk. Stir with a wooden spoon to combine. With your hands, gather the dough into a ball.

2 Turn the dough out onto a lightly floured work surface and knead for 10 minutes or until smooth and elastic. Place in a lightly oiled bowl. Cover with plastic wrap and stand in a warm place for 1 hour or until doubled in size.

3 Preheat the oven to 200°C (400°F/Gas 6). Lightly oil two large baking trays. Divide the dough into 12 even portions. Roll six of the portions into 30 cm (12 inch) lengths. Twist three of these into spiral shapes. Make the other three lengths into knot shapes. Place onto the trays.

4 Take another 3 portions and divide each into three little balls. Place three little balls close together like a caterpillar on the trays. Repeat with the other little balls.

5 Roll the remaining portions into neat balls and place onto the trays. Stand in a warm place for 20 minutes. Brush all the rolls with the extra milk and sprinkle with either poppy or sesame seeds. Use a small sharp knife to make a couple of slashes on top of the round rolls. Bake for 15 minutes or until golden.

GARLIC AND HERB
pretzels

MAKES 12 | **PREP TIME** 30 MINS + 1 HOUR 10 MINS RISING | **COOKING TIME** 15 MINS

125 ml (4^1/2 fl oz/^{1}/2 cup) **lukewarm water**
1 teaspoon **instant dried yeast**
1 teaspoon **caster (superfine) sugar**
1 teaspoon **cooking salt**
300 g (10^1/2 oz/2 cups) **plain bread (strong) flour**
2 tablespoons **olive oil**
1 **garlic clove**, crushed
3 tablespoons finely chopped **flat-leaf (Italian) parsley**
olive oil, extra, to brush
sea salt flakes, to sprinkle

1 Combine the water, yeast, sugar and salt in a bowl. Stand for 10 minutes or until the mixture is frothy. Place the flour in a mixing bowl and make a well in the centre. Add the yeast mixture, olive oil, garlic and parsley. Stir with a wooden spoon to combine. With your hands, gather the dough into a ball.

2 Turn the dough out onto a lightly floured work surface and knead for 10 minutes or until smooth and elastic. Place in a lightly oiled bowl, cover with plastic wrap and stand in a warm place for 1 hour or until doubled in size.

3 Preheat the oven to 200°C (400°F/Gas 6). Lightly oil two baking trays. Divide the dough into 12 portions. Roll each portion into a 30 cm (12 inch) long sausage. Curl the ends into the centre, cross over and press together. Place onto the trays and brush with the oil. Sprinkle with the salt flakes. Stand in a warm place for 10 minutes.

4 Bake for 15 minutes or until golden. Transfer to a wire rack to cool. Serve warm or at room temperature.

MINI PUMPKIN
quickbreads

MAKES 8 | **PREP TIME** 20 MINS | **COOKING TIME** 15–18 MINS

375 g (13 oz/2$^{1}/_{2}$ cups) **self-raising flour**
1 teaspoon **cooking salt**
30 g (1 oz) **butter**, chilled and chopped
1 **egg**
60 ml (2 fl oz/$^{1}/_{4}$ cup) **milk**
260 g (9$^{1}/_{4}$ oz/1 cup) cooked, mashed **pumpkin (winter squash)**
35 g (1$^{1}/_{4}$ oz/$^{1}/_{4}$ cup) finely grated **parmesan cheese**
2 tablespoons chopped **chives**
1 tablespoon **pepitas (pumpkin seeds)**

1 Preheat the oven to 200°C (400°F/Gas 6). Line a large baking tray with baking paper. Sift the flour and salt into a large mixing bowl. Add the butter and use your fingertips to rub it in until combined. Make a well in the centre.

2 Whisk the egg and milk together and add to the bowl along with the pumpkin, parmesan and chives. Use a wooden spoon to combine. Lightly flour your hands and divide the mixture into eight equal portions.

3 Shape each portion into neat rounds and place onto the tray. Brush with water and sprinkle with the pepitas. Bake for 15–18 minutes or until golden. Serve warm with a sprinkle of your favourite cheese.

For the mashed pumpkin, you will need about 450 g (1 lb) raw, peeled pumpkin.

COWBOY rolls

MAKES 16 | **PREP TIME** 25 MINS | **COOKING TIME** 15 MINS

375 g (13 oz/2¹/₂ cups) **self-raising flour**
60 g (2¹/₄ oz/¹/₃ cup) **polenta (cornmeal)**
60 g (2¹/₄ oz) **butter**, chopped
185 ml (6 fl oz/³/₄ cup) **milk**
90 g (3¹/₄ oz/¹/₃ cup) bought **taco sauce**
75 g (2¹/₂ oz/³/₄ cup) finely grated **cheddar cheese**

1 Preheat the oven to 200°C (400°F/Gas 6). Line a large baking tray with baking paper. Sift the flour into a mixing bowl and stir in the polenta. Add the butter and use your fingertips to rub it until combined. Make a well in the centre.

2 Pour the milk into the well. Using a non-serrated knife, stir until the mixture is almost combined. With your hands, gather the dough into a ball. Turn onto a lightly floured work surface and gently knead until almost smooth. Roll the dough out onto a sheet of baking paper to a rectangle, about 32 x 22 cm (12³/₄ x 8¹/₂ inches).

3 Cut the dough in half lengthways. Cut seven triangles from each portion of the dough, with a base of about 8 cm (3¹/₄ inches). You will have a 'half' triangle left at each end — press these together to make two more whole triangles. Spread a little taco sauce over each and sprinkle with cheese.

4 Starting from the wide end, roll up each triangle so that the point ends up on the outside. Place onto the tray, with the point tucked under. Bake for 15 minutes or until golden. Leave on the tray for a couple of minutes, then transfer to a wire rack to cool.

These are great served with guacamole.

PESTO
pastries

MAKES 12 | **PREP TIME** 15 MINS + 20 MINS CHILLING | **COOKING TIME** 15 MINS

2 sheets frozen **puff pastry**, thawed
2^1/$_2$ tablespoons **sun-dried tomato pesto**
2^1/$_2$ tablespoons **basil pesto**

1 Preheat the oven to 200°C (400°F/Gas 6). Line two baking trays with baking paper. Lay out the pastry sheets on a work surface so that one edge overlaps by about 1 cm (1/2 inch) to make a rectangle. Press the edge together firmly to join. Spread tomato pesto onto one side and basil pesto onto the other.

2 Fold the pastry about 5 cm (2 inches) over on each side, then repeat folding each side until they meet in the middle. Chill for 20 minutes to firm the pastry.

3 Use a sharp knife to cut the pastry into 12 slices. Arrange, cut-side up, onto the trays and bake for 15 minutes or until golden and crisp.

These taste best straight from the oven or eaten on the day of baking. You can prepare the pastries a day ahead and bake when hungry. Store the prepared pastries, covered with plastic wrap, in the fridge.

VEGGIE
filo cups

MAKES 6 | **PREP TIME** 30 MINS | **COOKING TIME** 25 MINS

6 sheets **filo pastry**
olive oil spray
1 tablespoon **olive oil**
1 **onion**, chopped
1 large **zucchini (courgette)**, chopped
1 **red capsicum (pepper)**, chopped
1 small **eggplant (aubergine)**, chopped
2 **garlic cloves**, crushed
3 **tomatoes**, chopped

1 Preheat the oven to 180°C (350°F/Gas 4). Lightly grease six 185 ml (6 fl oz/¾ cup capacity) muffin holes with oil. Spray a sheet of filo with oil and fold in half to make a rough square. Fold each corner into the centre of the square to make a smaller square. Ease the square into one of the muffin holes — let overhanging pastry stand above the rim. Repeat with the remaining filo sheets. Keep the filo sheets you aren't working with covered with a damp tea towel (dish towel) to prevent them drying out.

2 Bake for 10 minutes or until crisp and golden. Cool slightly in the tin, then carefully transfer to a wire rack to cool.

3 Meanwhile, heat the olive oil in a large, deep frying pan. Add the onion, zucchini, capsicum and eggplant and cook, stirring occasionally, for 10 minutes. Add the garlic and cook, stirring, for 1 minute. Stir in the tomato and cook for 15 minutes or until all the vegetables have softened. Season to taste with salt and pepper.

4 Gently press down the centre of the tart cases if they have puffed up too much and fill with the hot vegetable mixture. Serve straight away.

calzones

MAKES 4 | **PREP TIME** 25 MINS + 45 MINS RISING | **COOKING TIME** 15 MINS

80 ml ($2^1/_2$ fl oz/$^1/_3$ cup) **lukewarm water**
1 teaspoon **instant dried yeast**
1 teaspoon **caster (superfine) sugar**
1 pinch of **cooking salt**
150 g ($5^1/_2$ oz/1 cup) **plain (all-purpose) flour**
1 tablespoon **olive oil**
3 **short-cut bacon slices**, chopped and cooked
100 g ($3^1/_2$ oz) **chargrilled red capsicum (pepper)**, chopped
2 x 125 g ($4^1/_2$ oz) tins **corn kernels**, drained
60 ml (2 fl oz/$^1/_4$ cup) **tomato pasta sauce**
60 g ($2^1/_4$ oz/$^1/_2$ cup) grated **mozzarella cheese**
1 **egg**, lightly beaten

1 Combine the water, yeast, sugar and salt in a bowl and stand for 10 minutes or until frothy. Place the flour in a mixing bowl and make a well in the centre. Add the yeast mixture and olive oil. Stir with a wooden spoon to combine. With your hands, gather the dough into a ball.

2 Turn out onto a lightly floured work surface and knead for 5 minutes or until smooth and elastic. Place into a lightly oiled bowl, cover with plastic wrap and stand in a warm place for 45 minutes or until doubled in size.

3 Preheat the oven to 200°C (400°F/Gas 6). Grease a large baking tray. Punch the dough to expel the air and divide into 4 equal portions. Knead briefly, then roll out each portion on a lightly floured work surface to make a 12 cm ($4^1/_2$ inch) round.

4 Combine the bacon, capsicum, corn and pasta sauce in a bowl. Place one-quarter of the mixture onto each round and top with one-quarter of the cheese. Fold over to make a semicircle and pinch the edges to seal. Carefully place onto the tray and use a small sharp knife to slash the tops. Brush with the beaten egg and bake for 15 minutes or until golden.

CHICKEN AND CORN
cottage pies

MAKES 4 I **PREP TIME** 30 MINS I **COOKING TIME** 30 MINS

2 sheets frozen **shortcrust pastry**, thawed
30 g (1 oz) **butter**
1 small **onion**, finely chopped
1 tablespoon **plain (all-purpose) flour**
185 ml (6 fl oz/3/4 cup) **milk**
50 g (1³/4 oz/¹/2 cup) grated **cheddar cheese**
200 g (7 oz/1¹/2 cups) chopped **cooked chicken**
1 x 125 g (4¹/2 oz) tin **corn kernels**, drained
600 g (1 lb 5 oz) **sweet potato**, peeled and chopped
2 tablespoons **milk**, extra

1 Preheat the oven to 180°C (350°F/Gas 4). Lightly grease four deep 8 cm (3¹/4 inch) round loose-based tart tins. Using a saucer as a guide, cut two 15 cm (6 inch) rounds from each sheet of pastry. They will overlap slightly, so use a piece of leftover pastry to patch up the missing section. Ease into the tins and line the pastry with baking paper. Fill with dried rice or beans and place on a baking tray. Bake for 10 minutes. Remove the paper and rice and bake for a further 10 minutes. Cool in the tins.

2 Meanwhile, melt the butter in a saucepan over medium heat. Add the onion and cook for about 5 minutes or until softened. Stir in the flour and cook for 1 minute. Add the milk, a little at a time, stirring until well combined between each addition. Bring to the boil and cook for 1 minute, then stir in the cheese until melted. Stir in the chicken and corn.

3 Steam the sweet potato until very tender. Mash until smooth, then stir in the extra milk. Season to taste with salt and pepper.

4 Spoon the chicken mixture into the pastry cases. Pipe the mash onto the pies and bake for 10 minutes or until heated through.

SWEET

WHOOPIE pies

MAKES 8 | **PREP TIME** 25 MINS | **COOKING TIME** 13 MINS

125 g (4$^{1}/_{2}$ oz) **butter**, chopped
135 g (4$^{3}/_{4}$ oz /$^{2}/_{3}$ cup) **soft brown sugar**
1 teaspoon **natural vanilla extract**
1 **egg**
150 g (5$^{1}/_{2}$ oz /1 cup) **plain (all-purpose) flour**
75 g (2$^{1}/_{2}$ oz /$^{1}/_{2}$ cup) **self-raising flour**
35 g (1$^{1}/_{4}$ oz /$^{1}/_{3}$ cup) **unsweetened cocoa powder**
1 teaspoon **bicarbonate of soda (baking soda)**
185 ml (6 fl oz /$^{3}/_{4}$ cup) **milk**
20 **marshmallows**

1 Preheat the oven to 180°C (350°F/Gas 4). Line two large baking trays with baking paper. Using electric beaters, beat the butter, sugar and vanilla until light and creamy. Add the egg and beat well.

2 Sift the flours, cocoa powder and bicarbonate of soda together. Add to the butter mixture, along with the milk. Beat gently until evenly combined, scraping the side of the bowl occasionally. Drop heaped tablespoons of the mixture onto the trays and use the back of a spoon to spread each to make a 6 cm (2$^{1}/_{2}$ inch) round. Leave room around each for spreading (you may have to bake these in batches).

3 Bake for 12 minutes or until the cakes are just springy when gently touched. Remove half of the cakes from the trays and set aside. Turn the remaining cakes on the trays upside down. Use scissors to cut the marshmallows in half horizontally. Cover the cakes on the tray with marshmallows and return to the oven for 1 minute to soften.

4 Remove from the oven and place another cake on top to sandwich together. Leave to cool and set.

CHOCCY BUTTERFLY
cakes

MAKES 12 | **PREP TIME** 20 MINS | **COOKING TIME** 15 MINS

125 g (4^1/2 oz) **butter**, chopped
110 g (3^3/4 oz/^{1}/2 cup) **caster (superfine) sugar**
1 teaspoon **natural vanilla extract**
2 **eggs**
190 g (6^3/4 oz/1^1/4 cups) **self-raising flour**
35 g (1^1/4 oz/^{1}/3 cup) **unsweetened cocoa powder**
185 ml (6 fl oz/^{3}/4 cup) **milk**
50 g (1^3/4 oz/^{1}/3 cup) **dark chocolate melts**, melted
185 ml (6 fl oz/^{3}/4 cup) **cream**

1 Preheat the oven to 180°C (350°F/Gas 4). Line twelve 80 ml (2^1/2 fl oz/ ^{1}/3 cup capacity) muffin holes with paper cases. Using electric beaters, beat the butter, sugar and vanilla until light and creamy. Add the eggs, one at a time, beating well after each addition.

2 Sift the flour and cocoa powder together. Fold into the butter mixture along with the milk until just combined. Spoon into the cases. Bake for 15 minutes or until the cakes spring back when gently touched. Transfer to a wire rack to cool completely.

3 Place the melted chocolate into a small piping bag fitted with a small nozzle. Pipe 'antennae' onto a sheet of baking paper. Leave to set.

4 Using electric beaters, whip the cream until soft peaks form. Use a small sharp knife to cut the cake tops off, starting about 1 cm (1/2 inch) in from the edge. Dollop or pipe cream in the cut hollow of each cake. Cut the tops in half and put in place to form wings. Put the antennae in place to finish.

JAM THUMBPRINT
drops

MAKES 25 I **PREP TIME** 30 MINS I **COOKING TIME** 18 MINS

250 g (9 oz) **butter**, chopped and at room temperature
165 g (5^3/4 oz/^{3}/4 cup) **caster (superfine) sugar**
1 teaspoon **natural vanilla extract**
1 **egg yolk**
375 g (13 oz/2^1/2 cups) **plain (all-purpose) flour**
1 teaspoon **baking powder**
80 g (2^3/4 oz/^{1}/4 cup) **raspberry jam**

1 Preheat the oven to 170°C (325°F/Gas 3). Line two large baking trays with baking paper. Using electric beaters, beat the butter, sugar and vanilla until light and creamy. Add the egg yolk and beat until combined.

2 Sift the flour and baking powder over the butter mixture. Use a non-serrated knife to combine the mixture until it is evenly moistened and starts to form clumps. With your hands, gather the dough into a ball.

3 Roll slightly heaped tablespoons of the mixture into balls. Place onto the trays and flatten very slightly. Use your thumb, forefinger or the end of a round-handled wooden spoon to make deep indentations in the centre of each ball. Fill each hole with jam.

4 Bake for 18 minutes or until lightly golden. Leave the cookies on the trays for 5 minutes, then transfer to a wire rack to cool.

You can use whichever jam is your favourite, but choose one that doesn't have big fruit pieces in it. And try not to put too much jam in the holes.

BAKED doughnuts

MAKES 10 | **PREP TIME** 30 MINS + 1½ HOURS RISING | **COOKING TIME** 8–10 MINS

125 ml (4½ fl oz/½ cup) **lukewarm milk**
2 teaspoons **instant dried yeast**
55 g (2 oz/¼ cup) **caster (superfine) sugar**
300 g (10½ oz/2 cups) **plain (all-purpose) flour**, plus extra, for dusting
1 **egg**, lightly beaten
40 g (1½ oz) **butter**, melted
1 teaspoon **natural vanilla extract**
450 g (1 lb/3 cups) **icing (confectioners') sugar**, sifted
2½ tablespoons **hot water**
food colouring of your choice
lollies (candy) or **sprinkles**, to decorate

1 Whisk the milk, yeast and 1 teaspoon of the caster sugar together. Set aside for 5 minutes or until frothy. Combine the flour and remaining caster sugar in a bowl and make a well in the centre. Add the milk mixture, egg, butter and vanilla to the well. Use a wooden spoon to combine the mixture until it is evenly moistened. With your hands, gather the dough into a ball. Turn the dough out onto a lightly floured work surface and knead for 5 minutes or until smooth. Place in a lightly oiled bowl, cover with plastic wrap and set aside in a warm place for 1 hour or until doubled in size.

2 Punch the dough to expel the air and knead again until smooth. Roll out to 1.5 cm (⅝ inch) thick. Use a 7 cm (2¾ inch) round cutter to cut out rounds, then using a 3 cm (1¼ inch) cutter, cut a hole in the middle. Re-roll the scraps to cut out more doughnuts. Arrange on two trays lined with baking paper, leaving space between each one. Cover loosely with a lightly oiled sheet of plastic wrap. Set aside for 30 minutes to rise.

3 Preheat the oven to 190°C (375°F/Gas 5). Bake for 8–10 minutes or until golden. Transfer to a wire rack to cool.

4 Stir the icing sugar and water together until smooth. Stir in a few drops of colouring. Dip the doughnuts into the icing, allowing any excess to drip off. Place on a wire rack and decorate with lollies. Leave to set.

LITTLE FRESH
fruit tarts

MAKES 12 | **PREP TIME** 20 MINS + 10 MINS RESTING | **COOKING TIME** 15 MINS

150 g (5¹/₂ oz/1 cup) **plain (all-purpose) flour**
2 tablespoons **icing (confectioners') sugar**
75 g (2¹/₂ oz) **butter**, chopped
2 tablespoons **iced water**
250 ml (9 fl oz/1 cup) bought **thick custard**
fresh fruit, such as **berries, mandarin, star fruit** or **grapes**

1 Preheat the oven to 180°C (350°F/Gas 4). Lightly grease a 12-hole shallow round-based patty pan. Place the flour, icing sugar and butter in a food processor. Using the pulse button, process in short bursts until the mixture resembles breadcrumbs. Add the iced water and pulse again in short bursts until the mixture clumps together in small pieces. Be careful not to over-mix it.

2 Turn the dough out onto a sheet of baking paper and gather together with your hands into a ball. Roll out the dough on the paper with a lightly floured rolling pin to a 5 mm (¹/₄ inch) thickness. Use a 7 cm (2³/₄ inch) cutter to cut out rounds from the dough as close together as you can and place into the patty pan. Gently re-roll the dough scraps to cut out more rounds. Put in the fridge for 10 minutes to rest.

3 Prick the bases with a fork and bake for 15 minutes or until lightly golden. Cool slightly in pans, then transfer to a wire rack to cool completely. Fill each tart with a tablespoon of custard and top with your favourite fresh fruit.

CHOCOLATE
profiteroles

MAKES 12 I **PREP TIME** 35 MINS + 1 HOUR COOLING I **COOKING TIME** 20-25 MINS

30 g (1 oz) **butter**, chopped
125 ml (4^1/2 fl oz/^{1}/2 cup) **water**
75 g (2^1/2 oz/^{1}/2 cup) **plain (all-purpose) flour**
3 **eggs**, lightly beaten in a jug
100 g (3^1/2 oz) **dark chocolate**, melted
500 ml (17 fl oz/2 cups) bought **thick custard**

1 Preheat the oven to 200°C (400°F/Gas 6). Line two large baking trays with baking paper. Place the butter in a large saucepan and add the water. Cook over medium heat until the butter has melted and the mixture comes to the boil. With the pan still on the stove, sift the flour into the pan and stir with a wooden spoon for about 1 minute or until the mixture comes away from the side of the pan in a lump.

2 Transfer the mixture to a bowl and cool slightly, stirring to release the heat. Add the egg, a little bit at a time, beating well with electric beaters after each addition until the mixture is very thick and glossy. Drop slightly heaped tablespoons of the mixture onto the trays, leaving plenty of space between each one.

3 Bake for 20–25 minutes or until puffed and golden. Quickly swap trays from the top to bottom shelf halfway through cooking. When they are ready, use a skewer to pierce a small hole in each profiterole, return to the oven, turn off the heat, prop the door ajar and leave to cool for 1 hour.

4 Cut the profiteroles in half horizontally. Dip the tops in the melted chocolate and place upright on a wire rack to set. Spoon custard into the bottom halves and replace the tops.

ORANGE
yoyo cookies

MAKES 15 | **PREP TIME** 30 MINS | **COOKING TIME** 15 MINS

125 g (4^{1}/2 oz) **butter**, chopped and at room temperature
2 tablespoons **icing (confectioners') sugar**
1 teaspoon **natural vanilla extract**
115 g (4 oz/^{3}/4 cup) **plain (all-purpose) flour**
30 g (1 oz/^{1}/4 cup) **custard powder**
custard powder, extra, for dipping

FILLING
60 g (2^{1}/4 oz) **butter**, chopped and at room temperature
75 g (2^{1}/2 oz/^{1}/2 cup) **icing (confectioners') sugar**
2 teaspoons finely grated **orange zest**

1 Preheat the oven to 160°C (315°F/Gas 2–3). Line two baking trays with baking paper. Using electric beaters, beat the butter, icing sugar and vanilla until light and creamy. Use a non-serrated knife to mix in the flour and custard powder until the mixture starts to form clumps. With your hands, gather the dough into a ball.

2 Roll heaped teaspoons of the dough into small balls and place on the trays. Gently press each with a fork (first one way, then at right angles) to flatten out to make 3 cm (1¼ inch) rounds. Dip the fork in the extra custard powder to prevent it sticking. Bake for 15 minutes or until lightly browned underneath. Leave on the trays for 5 minutes, then transfer to a wire rack to cool completely.

3 To make the filling, use electric beaters to beat the butter and icing sugar until light and creamy. Beat in the orange zest. Spread or pipe filling onto half of the cookies, then sandwich with another cookie. Store in an airtight container for up to 3 days.

MINI
berry cakes

MAKES 6 | **PREP TIME** 25 MINS | **COOKING TIME** 20–25 MINS

225 g (8 oz/1^1/$_2$ cups) **self-raising flour**
220 g (7^3/$_4$ oz/1 cup) **caster (superfine) sugar**
125 ml (4^1/$_2$ fl oz/^{1}/$_2$ cup) **milk**
2 **eggs**
1 teaspoon **natural vanilla extract**
125 g (4^1/$_2$ oz) **butter**, melted and cooled
125 g (4^1/$_2$ oz/1 cup) **mixed berries** (fresh or frozen)

ICING
225 g (8 oz/1^1/$_2$ cups) **icing (confectioners') sugar**
30 g (1 oz) **butter**, softened
2^1/$_2$ tablespoons **boiling water**
icing flowers, to decorate

1 Preheat the oven to 180°C (350°F/Gas 4). Lightly grease six 200 ml (7 fl oz) capacity cake tins and line the bases with baking paper (or use six 185 ml (6 fl oz/^{3}/$_4$ cup) capacity muffin holes lined with paper cases). Sift the flour into a mixing bowl and stir in the sugar. Make a well in the centre.

2 Whisk the milk, eggs and vanilla together and add to the bowl along with the butter. Use a rubber spatula to combine, but don't overbeat. Fold in the berries. Spoon the mixture into the tins so they are three-quarters full. Bake for 20–25 minutes or until the cakes spring back when gently touched. Leave in the tins for 5 minutes, then turn out onto a wire rack to cool completely.

3 To make the icing, sift the icing sugar into a bowl. Add the butter and pour over the water. Stir until smooth. Transfer to a jug and slowly pour the icing onto the cakes, allowing it to run down the sides, then decorate.

RASPBERRY
cream horns

MAKES 16 | **PREP TIME** 30 MINS | **COOKING TIME** 10–15 MINS

2 sheets frozen **puff pastry**, thawed
75 g (2¹/2 oz/¹/3 cup) **demerara (raw) sugar**
100 g (3¹/2 oz/¹/3 cup) **raspberry jam**
250 ml (9 fl oz/1 cup) **cream**
small lollies (candy), to decorate

1 Preheat the oven to 200°C (400°F/Gas 6). Line two baking trays with baking paper and lightly oil 16 cream horn moulds. Cut each pastry sheet into 8 strips.

2 Hold the mould with the point on the right, and press an end of a pastry strip around the point. Carefully wind the pastry around the mould, working your way up to the wide end, overlapping the pastry slightly. Don't go all the way to the end.

3 Place the sugar on a plate and gently roll the pastry-lined cones in the sugar to coat. Place onto the trays, with the seam underneath so the pastry doesn't unwind during cooking. Bake for 10–15 minutes or until crisp and golden. Transfer to a wire rack until cool enough to handle, then gently pull out the moulds. Cool completely.

4 Stir the jam in a small bowl to make it runny. Using electric beaters, beat the cream until firm peaks form. Gently fold the jam through the cream to create streaks. Spoon into a piping bag fitted with a fluted nozzle. Pipe the jammy cream into the cream horns and place a lolly on top of each.

Cream horn moulds are small metal cones, available from kitchen shops and online. If you don't have enough moulds, cook these in batches.

KOOKY
cake pops

MAKES 24 | **PREP TIME** 1 HOUR + 30 MINS CHILLING | **COOKING TIME** 40 MINS

1 quantity **cake mixture** (see mini berry cakes, page 50)
3 tablespoons bought **vanilla frosting**
24 **popsicle sticks**
375 g (13 oz/2$^1/_2$ cups) **white chocolate melts**
2 x **12-hole egg cartons**
sprinkles, to decorate

1 Preheat the oven to 180°C (350°F/Gas 4). Lightly grease a 20 cm (8 inch) round cake tin and line the base with baking paper. Make up the cake mixture (but omit the berries) and spread into the tin. Bake for 40 minutes or until the cake springs back when gently touched in the centre. Leave in the tin for 5 minutes, then turn out onto a wire rack to cool completely.

2 Break up the cake in a mixing bowl and use your fingertips to crumble thoroughly. Add the frosting and mix in with your fingers until the mixture is very moist and sticky. Take slightly heaped tablespoons of the mixture and roll into firm balls. Press a popsicle stick into each ball and chill for 30 minutes.

3 Place the chocolate in a deep bowl and heat in the microwave until melted. Remove and stir until smooth. Turn the empty egg cartons upside down and cut a slit in the top of each egg holder. Carefully dip the cake ball into the chocolate, turning to coat evenly (tilt the bowl as needed). Let the excess chocolate drip back into the bowl.

4 Keep turning the cake pop so the chocolate starts to set evenly. As soon as it starts to thicken, decorate the pop all over with sprinkles (if you do it too soon, they will fall off). Stand the stick in the egg carton so the pop stands upright to set. Repeat with the remaining cake pops.

ROCKY ROAD
Cups

MAKES 15 | **PREP TIME** 25 MINS | **COOKING TIME** 20 MINS

150 g (5^1/2 oz/1 cup) **plain (all-purpose) flour**
35 g (1^1/4 oz/^{1}/3 cup) **unsweetened cocoa powder**
110 g (3^3/4 oz/^{1}/2 cup) **caster (superfine) sugar**
1 **wheat biscuit cereal**, such as Weet-Bix or Weetabix, crushed
1 **egg**, lightly beaten
125 g (4^1/2 oz) **butter**, melted and cooled

TOPPING
75 g (2^1/2 oz/^{1}/2 cup) **dried cranberries**
65 g (2^1/4 oz/1^1/2 cups) **pink** and **white mini marshmallows**
50 g (1^3/4 oz/^{2}/3 cup) **shredded coconut**
35 g (1^1/4 oz/1 cup) **puffed rice cereal**, such as Rice Bubbles
225 g (8 oz/1^1/2 cups) **white chocolate melts**, melted
m&m's, to decorate

1 Preheat the oven to 180°C (350°F/Gas 4). Lightly grease a 28 x 18 cm (11^1/4 x 7 inch) slice tin. Line with baking paper, making sure the paper extends over the two long sides. Sift the flour and cocoa powder into a bowl and stir in the sugar and crushed wheat biscuit cereal. Make a well in the centre. Add the egg and butter and mix together with a wooden spoon. Press into the prepared tin and smooth the surface. Bake for 20 minutes or until dry and set. Cool completely in the tin.

2 Use a 5 cm (2 inch) round cutter to cut 15 rounds from the base. Place each round into a paper case.

3 To make the topping, combine the cranberries, marshmallows, coconut and puffed rice cereal in a bowl. Pour over the chocolate and stir to combine. Spoon on top of the bases, sprinkle with m&m's and leave to set.

ANIMAL cookies

MAKES 18 | **PREP TIME** 40 MINS | **COOKING TIME** 12 MINS

150 g (5¹/2 oz) **butter**
100 g (3¹/2 oz /²/3 cup) **icing (confectioners') sugar**
1 teaspoon **natural vanilla extract**
1 **egg**
300 g (10¹/2 oz/2 cups) **plain (all-purpose) flour**
300 g (10¹/2 oz/2 cups) **icing (confectioners') sugar**, extra
2¹/2 tablespoons **hot water**
writing icing (frosting), to decorate

1 Preheat the oven to 160°C (315°F/Gas 2–3). Line two baking trays with baking paper. Using electric beaters, beat the butter and icing sugar until light and creamy. Beat in the vanilla and egg. Use a non-serrated knife to mix in the flour until evenly combined. With your hands, gather the dough into a ball and turn out onto a sheet of baking paper. Roll out to 1 cm (1/2 inch) thick.

2 Using 6–7 cm (2¹/2–2³/4 inch) animal-shaped cutters, cut the dough into shapes. Gently re-roll the dough scraps and cut out more shapes. Place onto the trays, and bake for about 12 minutes or until golden underneath (they will still be pale on top). Transfer to a wire rack to cool completely.

3 Sift the extra icing sugar into a bowl. Add the hot water and stir until smooth. Dip each cookie, face down, into the icing, allowing the excess to drip away. Carefully turn back upright and place onto a wire rack to set. Decorate with writing icing as desired.

You can store these cookies in an airtight container, in between sheets of baking paper, in a cool, dry place for up to 3 days.

SPARKLY
meringue kisses

MAKES 18 | **PREP TIME** 25 MINS + COOLING | **COOKING TIME** 2 HOURS

2 **egg whites**
110 g (3³/4 oz/¹/2 cup) **caster (superfine) sugar**
2 teaspoons **cornflour (cornstarch)**
1 teaspoon **natural vanilla extract**
1 tablespoon **decorating sugar crystals**, to sprinkle
100 g (3¹/2 oz/²/3 cup) **white chocolate melts**
food colourings of your choice

1 Preheat the oven to 100°C (200°F/Gas ¹/2). Lightly oil two baking trays and line with baking paper. Using electric beaters, beat the egg whites until soft peaks form. Add the sugar gradually, about 1 tablespoon at a time, beating until dissolved before you add more. Keep beating until the sugar is all added and the meringue is firm and glossy. Sprinkle the cornflour and vanilla over and beat briefly to combine.

2 Transfer the mixture to a piping bag fitted with a 1 cm (¹/2 inch) fluted nozzle. Pipe the mixture onto the trays to make 3 cm (1¹/4 inch) rounds, leaving plenty of space in between. Sprinkle with the decorating sugar crystals. Bake for 2 hours, then turn the oven off and leave to cool completely.

3 Place the chocolate in a heatproof bowl and place over a saucepan of just-simmering water. Stand for about 3 minutes until soft and melted, then stir with a metal spoon until smooth. Divide between smaller, warmed bowls. Add a few drops of food colouring to each to tint as desired and stir to combine. Spread onto a meringue, and sandwich together with another meringue. Place onto a wire rack to set. Repeat with the remaining meringues and chocolate.

INDEX

A

animal cookies **58**

B

baked doughnuts **42**

breads

cheesy twists **12**
cowboy rolls **24**
dinner rolls **19**
garlic and herb
    pretzels **20**
ham and pineapple
    scrolls **11**
mini pumpkin
    quickbreads **23**
pesto pastries **27**

C

cake pops, kooky **54**

cakes

choccy butterfly cakes **38**
kooky cake pops **54**
mini berry cakes **50**
whoopie pies **37**

calzones **31**
cheesy twists **12**
chicken and corn cottage
    pies **32**
choccy butterfly cakes **38**

chocolate

choccy butterfly cakes **38**
chocolate profiteroles **46**
kooky cake pops **54**
rocky road cups **57**
whoopie pies **37**

chocolate profiteroles **46**

cookies

animal cookies **58**
jam thumbprint drops **41**
orange yoyo cookies **49**

cowboy rolls **24**

D

dinner rolls **19**
doughnuts, baked **42**

G

garlic and herb pretzels **20**

H

ham and pineapple scrolls **11**

J

jam thumbprint drops **41**
jungle muffins **15**

K

kooky cake pops **54**

L

little fresh fruit tarts **45**

M

meringue kisses, sparkly **61**
mini berry cakes **50**
mini pumpkin quickbreads **23**
muffins, jungle **15**

O

orange yoyo cookies **49**

P

pesto pastries **27**

pies

chicken and corn cottage
    pies **32**
veggie filo cups **28**
whoopie pies **37**

pretzels, garlic and herb **20**

R

raspberry cream horns **53**
rocky road cups **57**

rolls

cowboy rolls **24**
dinner rolls **19**

S

sausage rolls, so-easy **16**
scrolls, ham and pineapple **11**
so-easy sausage rolls **16**
sparkly meringue kisses **61**

T

tarts, little fresh fruit **45**

V

veggie filo cups **28**

W

whoopie pies **37**

Published in 2011 by Hardie Grant Books

Hardie Grant Books (Australia)
Ground Floor, Building 1
658 Church Street
Richmond, Victoria 3121
www.hardiegrant.com.au

Hardie Grant Books (UK)
Second Floor, North Suite
Dudley House, Southampton Street
London WC2E 7HF
www.hardiegrant.co.uk

Publisher: Paul McNally
Editor: Belinda So
Series designer: Lauren Camilleri
3D imaging: Ben Hutchings
Photographer: Andre Martin
Stylist: Jane Collins
Recipe writing: Tracy Rutherford
Production manager: Penny Sanderson

Cataloguing-in-Publication data is available from the National Library
of Australia.

ISBN 9 781 742 701 493

Colour reproduction by Splitting Image Colour Studio
Printed in China by 1010 Printing International Limited